lemons to lemonade

Little Ways to Sweeten up Life's Sour Moments

addie johnson

Conari Press

First published in 2010 by
Red Wheel/Weiser, LLC

With offices at:
500 Third Street, Suite 230
San Francisco, CA 94107
www.redwheelweiser.com

ISBN: 978-1-57324-469-5
Library of Congress Cataloging-in-Publication Data
available upon request.

Cover and text design by Jessica Dacher.
Production Editor: Michele Kimble
Proofreader: Katherine Wright
Typeset in Baufy and Exuberance Primary.

Printed in Hong Kong
GWP
10 9 8 7 6 5 4 3 2 1

Contents

4 Introduction: When life hands you lemons, make lemonade.

6 Sweet and Sour: How You Look at Things

28 Simple Pleasures and Hidden Treasures

46 Happy, Healthy, Having a Blast

74 The Magic of Making Do and Making Things Better

102 Love and Affection

128 Thanksgiving Every Day

Introduction

When life hands you lemons, make lemonade.

Lemons are my favorite fruit. But even I can't sit down, slice open a lemon and dig in. A lemon is a fruit that has to become something else, enhance something, change something, make something happen. Can you think of another fruit that is almost completely inedible on its own, that becomes so divine in combination and transformation? Lemon meringue pie, lemon bars and cookies, lemon garnishing seafood or squeezed into sauces, lemon in fresh hot tea or squeezed into a pitcher of sweet iced tea. Not to mention fresh lemonade, that sweet and sour masterpiece that can change your life on a hot summer day.

What about those metaphorical lemons that life is bound to hand you now and then? Acidic, sour, trying times that you just can't seem to enjoy or digest. The most successful and happy among us never miss out on a chance to turn sour into sweet, hard times into learning experiences. While it may not be easy, we know that seeing those lemons as pure potential is the way to go. Adversity spurs creativity; challenge breeds success.

When you're feeling surrounded by useless lemons, never forget that you have some choices. When you're stuck in a difficult time, you can change your outlook and your circumstances, you can stay healthy and surround yourself with love, you can seek out and find the hidden treasure all around you in everyday things, and, perhaps most importantly, you can figure out how to be grateful for any and everything that comes your way. And you never know, maybe all it will take is a little water, sugar, and ice before you're feeling much, much better.

Sweet and Sour:
How You Look
at Things

Positivity

Did anyone ever tell you the glass is half full? Somebody told me once it depends whether you're pouring or drinking. Seriously, though, if you can figure out how to get optimistic and stay that way, you're home free. I'm not saying your problems are over, but simply looking at the world through rose-colored specs means that half your problems will look like exciting challenges, and the other half you'll probably realize aren't problems at all, just facts of life.

"It isn't what you have, or who you are,
or where you are, or what you are
doing that makes you happy or unhappy.
It is what you think about."

Dale Carnegie

I can think of people who have everything they could ever want and are still miserable. I can think of people just scraping by whose joy for life overflows onto everyone around them. Sometimes we take for granted the great pleasure we can take from very little things. Sometimes, too, we forget to give ourselves permission to enjoy over-the-top abundance, as if we somehow didn't deserve it. Most important, life is best when we set our judgments aside and savor the moment of whatever it is that the universe is dishing out, in big or small servings.

We're surrounded by beauty of all kinds. It can perk us up, calm us down, and even heal our bodies and souls. Getting attuned to this splendor is a great way to pass the time. It's time to shine up your sense of wonder and see the world in a new light. Make some new discoveries, and don't forget to pass them on through the magic of your own creativity.

Stop trying so hard. The harder you try to make yourself happy, or the more you focus on "being happy" for its own sake, without connecting it to actions in your life, the more it eludes you. Get out there and do it!

Magic

"Whatever you do, or dream you can, begin it. Boldness has genius and power and magic in it."

Johann Wolfgang von Goethe

More Laughing

Somebody told me that an average kindergartner laughs 300 times a day, while an adult averages seventeen times. This makes me want to be a kindergarten teacher.

Laughing at Yourself

Persnickety, controlling, stiff. I catch myself in this mode and I have to laugh. More fun to be the wild, goofy child poking fun at my uptight self.

Nothing but the Truth

"My way of joking is telling the truth; that is the funniest joke in the world."

George Bernard Shaw

Some people are tough customers, whether they're actual customers, bosses, employees, friends, or even family. Don't let it drain your energy. Figure out the minimum contact you can have, make it as pleasant as possible, and move on. Don't let anybody sap your energy.

Wisdom

"Be happy. It's one way
of being wise."

Sidonie Gabrielle

Creativity

The spark of creativity is life's first and greatest gift to us; we're conceived in that spark. And we have the chance to create every day, even in how we look at the world around us. We also get to bear witness to that spark in others through literature, scientific discoveries, music, and painting. If we pay attention, we can notice it in nature all around us: a perfect spider web, the formation of ice crystals on the windowpane, even a close examination of our own animal natures. Creation brings us joy, awe, and often a much needed new perspective.

Bugs

Ever bite into an apple with a worm? Make the best of it by remembering that even things we sometimes think are gross are really, truly wonderful. Spiders are good luck. Worms help plants grow. Bugs as part of the ecosystem, bugs making honey and silk, bugs eating peskier bugs, and so much more. It's a good exchange for a couple of wormy apples, or for those twelve mosquito bites I get every summer.

Butterfly Hunting

"Happiness is like a butterfly, which when pursued, is always just beyond your grasp, but which, if you will sit down quietly, may alight upon you."

Nathaniel Hawthorne

"The lemon tree has the reputation of tolerating very infertile, very poor soil."

Julia F. Morton

A Sense of Purpose

You may think that some work is beneath you, or that people are demeaned by having certain jobs. There are several ways to look at work you may not be excited about doing. You can feel demoralized or bitter about doing repetitious work that does not challenge or excite you, or you can find a sense of purpose in what you do. You can see your efforts in relation to the overall effect they are having as an essential part of the whole. Your sense of worth is in your own hands.

"We choose our joys
and sorrows long before
we experience them."

Kahlil Gibran

The Pursuit of Happiness

I've come to the conclusion (and I ain't the first or the last to come to it, let me tell you) that after the basic needs of survival are met, the pursuit of happiness is the most important thing we do in our lives. Why else would we spend so much time thinking about it, making art about it, hoping and wishing and planning for it?

Mind Over Matter

"Most folks are about as happy
as they make up their minds to be."

Abraham Lincoln

Infinity and Imagination

The full reach of infinity may be beyond our imagination,
but imagination itself is infinite.

As you wander through your life, friend,
whatever be your goal,
keep your eyes upon the donut
and not upon the hole.

Simple Pleasures
and Hidden
Treasures

Happiness is all around us. We can't create it and we can't micromanage it. You can't force yourself to be happier. You can only discover it. The best way I know to do that is to put yourself in the path of happy accidents by doing what you love with purpose and staying open and aware to the possibility of happiness beyond your wildest dreams. Too often we hide away the treasure of our own happiness as if there's a limited supply, and we forget that life will bring plenty more for us if we only let it.

Seeing Anew

There are plenty of magic tricks and scientific studies that prove that if we expect to see something, that's pretty much what we'll see, even if it's not really there. The same thing happens in our lives: we see the same thing every day, and we shut off the part of ourselves that's on the lookout for the new and interesting, so sometimes we pass it by altogether. Can you vow to see something new every day?

Sound Advice

"Always act your shoe size."
Anon

Cheap Thrills

Low on cash? Looking for a good way to have a blast or a nice way to calm down? Simple pleasures are the way to go for cheap thrills: going sledding; buying someone a single rose; driving with the windows down on a curvy road with your favorite song blasting; going wedding dress shopping (even if you're already married or have no intention of getting married anytime soon); enjoying the free day at the museum, botanical garden, boardwalk, aquarium; eating chocolate chips right out of the bag; taking in the view at the top of a high building.

Cheap Chills

Sometimes we forget how taking time to do the simplest things can calm us down better than any spa treatment. Drinking warm milk with honey, collecting pinecones or autumn leaves, fishing (or sitting in the boat all day), knitting or crocheting, putting pictures in an album, tossing a ball around, eating an ice cream cone, skipping rocks.

Got the bluey blues? Feel better fast by indulging in aromatherapy: lavender, chamomile, citrus, cinnamon. Smells are some of the most powerful stimulants and soothers. Or try color therapy: Orange peps you up, green calms you down, and silver is mentally cleansing. Get out your paintbrush.

I think gardeners are artists, scientists, even alchemists. They channel light and water into a canvas of plants, trees, and flowers and create a landscape for every mood. And don't forget the joy of good clean garden dirt so thick under your fingernails that no amount of scrubbing will get it out.

Did you know that lemonade helps keep the flowers in potted plants fresher for longer?

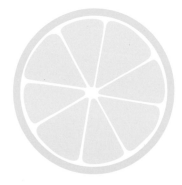

Friends

True friendship is at the core of any happy life. If our family is our root system, our friends are our fellow branches. We're all striving together, supporting one another, providing shade and comfort.

Best Friends

A dog will be there whenever you call, always be thrilled to see you come through the door, sit by your feet or on your lap through your darkest moods, jump at the chance to join you whenever you go out. What could be better?

Songs from Your Parents' Generation

No matter your age, there is something wonderful about the music your parents listened to. Even if you made mean gagging sounds about it as a teenager, chances are that now you have at least a little nostalgic appreciation. Whether it's Bob Dylan and Joni Mitchell, the Four Tops and Aretha, Elton John and Iggy Pop, Frank Sinatra, or Elvis Presley, it can be comforting to relive your childhood through music.

Sharing Headphones

The other day I saw a mother and her maybe six-year-old daughter on the subway, each with one earpiece, jamming out and dancing so hard to the music they were both hearing that the little girl's earpiece would fall out from time to time. They'd laugh hysterically until she got it back in, and then they would go back to their boogie.

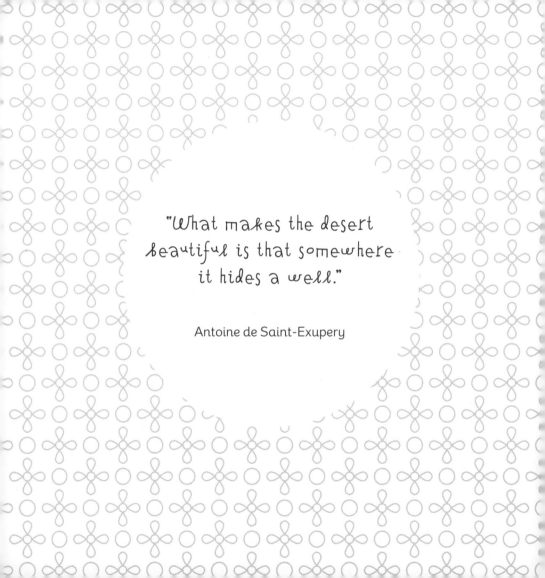

"What makes the desert
beautiful is that somewhere
it hides a well."

Antoine de Saint-Exupery

Sweet Tooth

To indulge, or not to indulge? Chocolate is one of life's great treasures, and that's just the tip of the iceberg-sized sundae. Plus, you never know what's coming next. As Erma Bombeck once said, "Seize the moment. Remember all those women on the Titanic who waved off the dessert cart."

Through a Child's Eyes

Kids are really good at making the best of what they've got, discovering hidden joys, and imagining whole new worlds. We can take a few cues from them.

Curiosity about What Things Mean and How They Work. Why do we have to move on from the "why?" phase of life? Sure, it can get annoying when the response to every single thing you say is "Why? Why? Why?" But we could all stand to ask "Why?" a little more often.

A Quasi-Maniacal Love of Trains, Dogs, Ponies, and/or Princesses. "A dog! A dog! A dog! A dog!" my son yells until I acknowledge that yes, there is a dog coming down the sidewalk toward us. What makes you so excited you want to shout about it in public?

Playing Dress-up. When's the last time you put on your best costume jewelry and threw a tea party?

Sharing. It's tough to share sometimes, but the results are be rewarding in unexpected ways.

Attention to Detail. Every mud puddle deserves a thorough investigation.

Doing Things Just for the Sake of Doing Them. Jumping jacks, silly faces, knock-knock jokes, holding hands, sticking peanuts up your nose. Okay, scratch that last one or you might end up in the emergency room on the pointy end of a pair of pliers.

Horizons

Take in your horizons by lifting your eyes off of the ground in front of you and put your focus far out in front of you. Of course you can't keep your eyes fixed off in the distance— you're going to look at other things, make eye contact with a passerby, notice something shiny on the path ahead of you. But make the horizon your default position, and you will inter- act with the world in a different way. Open yourself up to seeing outside of the little bubble of sensation that surrounds you.

Permission Granted

I sometimes catch myself thinking I practically need a note from home to really enjoy things. Maybe I feel I don't deserve it, or I'm always thinking about what I should be doing instead, but I think it's time to write a permission slip for a lot of things: eating a special treat, going for a long walk, having fun even when I've got a huge to-do list.

Happy,
Healthy, Having
a Blast

I'm looking for the fountain of youth. Is it eating less of this, more of that? Is it family? Nature? Nurture? Stress levels? I can feel my stress level rising as I try to parse out exactly what is good or bad for me by the measure of the most recent scientific reports. Agh—forget it! I'm just going to go back to the basics and assume I'm adding years to my life by eating wonderful food, laughing hysterically, staying close to friends and family, and keeping busy in mind and body. And if I'm not, then at least I'm enjoying the heck out of whatever youth I've got left.

Hope

"He who has health, has hope.
And he who has hope,
has everything."

Proverb

Laughter Is the Best Medicine

Diagnosed with a rare disease and given only months to live, scientist Norman Cousins checked himself into a hotel room and took massive doses of vitamin C and watched funny movies and television shows all day long. And it worked. For every ten minutes of belly laughs, he got two hours pain free. He lived far beyond anyone's expectations and ignited more serious study of laughter as medicine.

Did You Know?

Laughter can boost blood flow as much as light exercise or drugs that lower cholesterol.

Guess What Else?

There's some good evidence that laughter can boost the immune system, as well as clean toxins out of the lungs and blood stream.

Uniting the Brain

In order to get a joke, we need to use both sides of our brain: the left hemisphere understands the verbal content of a joke and the right figures out whether it's funny or not. So laughing keeps our brains young and fit.

Painkiller

Laughter releases endorphins that are more potent than equiv-
alent amounts of morphine. What's more, you don't need to go
to rehab to quit laughing if you get hooked.

A strong, healthy family provides the foundation for a wonderful life. An insane, dysfunctional family forms the basis of a
best-selling novel.

Birthdays

It's fun to have something you always do on your birthday, whether it's drinking a toast in your honor, eating angel food cake, or getting spanked once for each year you've been kicking around this planet.

Pink Lemonade Pie

My friend Julie's family has a favorite guilty pleasure pick-me-up, invented by her grandmother Betty Loftesness:

Pink Lemonade Pie

1 (6 oz.) can pink lemonade

1 can condensed milk

1 small Cool Whip or $1/2$ pint cream, whipped

1 graham cracker pie crust

Mix together lemonade and milk. Fold in the whipped topping. Pour into graham cracker crust. Freeze for 2 to 3 hours.

Basic Needs

"As far as living a
healthy, happy life goes,
I hold loving and being
loved right up there with
fresh air and water."

Oprah Winfrey

Down to the Seeds

My father used to eat an apple all the way down to the seeds and the stem. He would finish off every edible piece, even the core. That's the way to live, it seems to me.

Your Birthright

Don't forget that you have the map that will lead you to more happiness than you can ever imagine, and you've had it forever—it's your birthright. Happiness doesn't care how much money you have or the circumstances you were born into. Your treasure map goes where you go; it's printed on your face and in your fingerprints, waiting for you to unlock its potential.

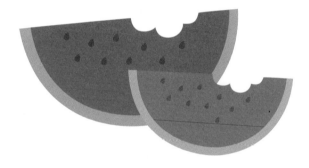

Have fun on your search for the sunny side, and don't forget to enjoy the journey. Life is sweet—yes, your life—if you just look at what's in front of your face.

Meditation

More and more scientific studies are confirming the benefits of the relaxed mindfulness of meditation. However you choose to do it, through prayer, yoga, mantras, or just sitting quietly, you're probably altering your body and brain for the better.

The Fountain of Youth?

If you want to keep a spring in your step and a twinkle in your eye, change your routine. Drive a different route to work, switch your right and left hands for everyday activities, eat dessert first, and wear your pajamas to work. Wait, no, that last one might get you in more trouble than it's worth.

Mental Pick-Me-Ups

Get the cranial juices flowing by practicing your Spanish verbs, or reciting the one sonnet you remember from high school, or even just thinking of ten words that rhyme with train. Anything to mix up your routine and send your brain a signal that it had better pick up the pace and get with the program.

Drink a Glass of Water

Looking for another way to see that the glass is half full? Did you know that 50 to 65 percent of your body weight is water? So you yourself are literally half full, plus some. Only problem is, you're always losing it—sweating, breathing, etc. Getting dehydrated can cause all kinds of problems, starting with being cranky and ending with keeling over. So hoist a full glass of the clear stuff whenever you can.

Taking the Stairs

"A man's health can be judged
by which he takes two
at a time—pills or stairs."

Joan Welsh

Spinal Alignment

Get thee to the chiropractor and come out feeling like a million bucks.

Get Upside Down

Reverse the effects of gravity for a moment. Hang on the monkey bars, do a headstand, ride a rollercoaster, or just try to touch your nose to your knees by bending down from a standing position. Hang there for a while and let the blood rush to your head.

Little Rewards

When you have a long and difficult task, reward yourself at every step. Not with a shopping spree or a new car, but with an apple, or a walk, or a piece of dark chocolate.

Keepsake

"Treasure the love you receive above all. It will survive long after your good health has vanished."

Og Mandino

Sunday Dinner

Whether your family is two people or thirty, it's wonderful to honor the tradition of getting everybody together for dinner once a week. Play the game of "Thorns and Roses," where everyone takes a turn telling a thorny thing and a rosy thing that happened in their day or week.

Walking

How often do you go out walking after dinner? City, country, or small town, there's something magical about walking every night after the sun goes down. Walking off the heaviness in your stomach, listening to the din of courting insects, looking in on scenes from the lives of your neighbors through their bright picture windows.

Get Some Sunlight

Get out there and boost your vitamin D. My husband's grand-mother swears by sitting in her lawn chair for twenty minutes every day.

Playing Your Part

"I think of life itself now as a wonderful play that I've written for myself, and so my purpose is to have the utmost fun playing my part."

Shirley MacLaine

The Magic of
making Do and
making Things
Better

You cannot poof yourself happy. And nobody else can either—no fairy godmother or perfect imagined spouse, no guru or fitness instructor. If you got everything you wanted (or thought you wanted)—poof—right now, you'd certainly feel happy for a little while. But scientists who study this stuff, and spiritual leaders, and the wise old lady who lives across the street all know one thing: feeling happy doesn't come from getting everything you think you want for nothing. It comes from dreaming about your goals and working to reach them. And it comes from paying attention to the little things in life that trigger a feeling of happiness—if you let them. It's great when the outcome of your efforts is what you want, but that's all really icing on the cake.

People in the worst situations still find a way to laugh. In fact, some would argue that we need laughter most when we're at our lowest point. They say laughter is the best medicine, to which I would also add it's the best way to bond with friends, the best pick-me-up, the best ice breaker, the best tension diffuser, and the best way to get through tough times. So have a giggle or a chuckle, a chortle or a snort, and get on with it.

"I believe if life
gives you lemons make
lemonade . . . then find
someone that life gave
vodka to and have a party."

Ron White

Bravery

What if I told you it's better to face the worst than to protect yourself from the sort-of-bad? I know, you don't believe me. Neither do I, a lot of the time. But it's still true.

The Gift of Failure

"Learn from the mistakes of others.
You can't live long enough to make
them all yourself."

Eleanor Roosevelt

Your Own Standard of Success

It can be tough in today's world to have an alternative standard of success. The media bombards us with images of people whom we're told have made it to the top. Our families have their own ideas of what we should do. It takes some courage, but defining and pursuing your own standard of success is worth it. Then no matter what your situation looks like to other people, you'll know that you're on the path to the life you've always dreamed about.

A Plan for Success

"To achieve great things,
two things are needed:
a plan, and not quite
enough time."

Leonard Bernstein

The Ingredients

There's no set recipe for success, but these ingredients certainly can't hurt.

Perseverance: Keep at it! There's no other way to know whether you can accomplish what you think you can.

Innovation: Redefine the landscape of your field. It can come to you in a moment, but is often the result of a lot of preparation—a miraculous new approach to an old problem.

Caring for Others: In simple, everyday ways and in dramatic, save-the-world ways like developing a new vaccine. If helping people is your focus, you can't go wrong.

Tackling Challenges: Biting off a little bit more than you think you can chew and pushing through problems as they come.

Resilience: Bounce back. Never let difficulty dull your happiness.

Faith: Knowing in your heart of hearts *this is right*.

Happiness comes from living a life that you feel is meaning-ful to you and enjoying the work you choose do. If you can find that sense of purpose, you may even find that obstacles themselves, and your approach to them, are another source of satisfaction in your life. Reach out and grab your calling.

Chosen

You often hear amazing, satisfied, courageous people say, "I had no idea I would be doing what I'm doing today. My life chose me."

Some people report the feeling that their calling found them, rather than the other way around. How can your life choose you? People may think it's luck or happenstance when opportunities knock on their door (or knock them down flat). But I believe that to make choices that will affect your life for the better, you must relinquish control. You must find a frame of mind from which you can make real choices, and that requires that you be in the moment, ready to evaluate the facts of your life honestly.

One problem that many of us overachievers face is our ability to plan and organize *ad nauseum*. We're relying too heavily on our left brain, which makes lists and generates orderly outcomes. Sometimes we have to put a muzzle on our efficient left brain and let loose the messy troublemaker, the right brain. Put on some music, make a drawing of your problem without using any words, or try a solution you think might be out of your reach. The right brain takes creative leaps of imagination, sees the bigger picture, and is the divining rod that can help your life choose you.

From a bumper sticker:

"Attitude is the only disability."

Efforts and Results

Sometimes you give it your all and still come up short. Sometimes a well-placed single burst of energy pays huge dividends.

The "Aha!" Moment

Whether in science, art, poetry, history, or anything else, there is magic in new discoveries. Research has found that the majority of discoveries, even those that seem to come out of the blue, come from rearranging information that is already well known. It's like taking a thousand-piece puzzle and assembling it all out of order and yet ending up with a perfectly clear picture no one's ever seen before. Eureka!

Stick-to-itiveness

As Thomas Edison put it, "The three great essentials to achieve anything worthwhile are, first, hard work; second, stick-to-itiveness; third, common sense." Stick-to-itiveness. It's a great word but an even greater idea. Many of history's best success stories are thanks to sheer perseverance. Some people even think stick-to-itiveness will take you further than being talented, smart, or born rich. I tend to agree.

"Adversity is like a strong wind.
It tears away from us all but the things
that cannot be torn, so that we see
ourselves as we really are."

Arthur Golden

Easy

The happiest people I know face challenges willingly, with a strength and energy I admire, and they end up growing in their careers and as human beings as a result. Others rarely push themselves, doing variations on the same simple tasks over and over to make themselves feel good and look smart. Seems to me the short-term comfort of easy success isn't worth the price of long-term stagnation.

"Smooth seas do not make skillful sailors."

Proverb

Acting Like a Baby

What would the world be like if we all acted like babies, at least emotionally? Babies are excellent communicators long before they can talk. Adults are not always great receptors, but that's another story. Crying isn't only about communicating; it's about going through the emotion fully, and physically getting it out of your system. Then the slate is clean for the next learning experience as it comes down the pike. What a great way to live.

Sing the Blues

"For me, singing sad songs often has a way of healing a situation. It gets the hurt out in the open into the light, out of the darkness."

Reba McEntire

Your House, Your Rules

Our kids give us maybe the greatest chance we'll ever get to look at our own attitudes and actions with fresh eyes and make the changes we feel we need to. Think about the rules you want your kids to live by—do you live by them? Honesty, hard work, a good dose of play every day, playing fair? You tell them that actions speak louder than words, or to follow their dreams no matter what, or that you love them no matter how mad you get. Are you giving yourself the same unconditional love? The best parents I know really mean it when they say, "I just want my kids to be happy." When's the last time you held yourself to that same standard?

Accomplishments

I don't remember how tough it was to learn to read, or to talk, or to button buttons, and I just have a dim sense of struggling to learn to tie my shoes. But I know that big accomplishments start small, and that's pretty cool.

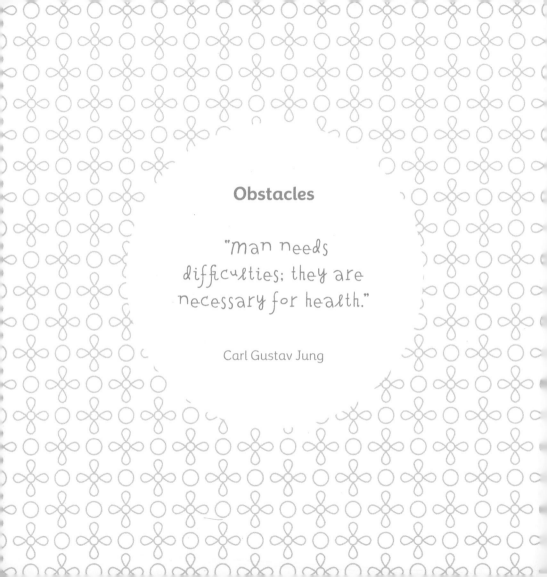

Obstacles

"Man needs
difficulties; they are
necessary for health."

Carl Gustav Jung

The Paradox of Control and Choice

When you're focused on control (of your life, your circumstances, your future) the only choices you are even allowing yourself to consider making are those that will help you maintain your sense of control. You are a slave to your own need to predict the future. The only way to make real, unfettered choices is to relinquish the need to know every possible outcome of the choices you make. Give it a try!

An act of creativity changes everything. Change can be a source of anxiety in our lives; we wonder how we will manage each new task or difficulty we face. But if we can embrace change as constant growth through creation of new things, we can be comforted and inspired by the unexpected. The masters of artistic expression show us this better than anyone. They turn words into worlds, musical notes into stories, brush-strokes into feelings, and they change our lives in the process. I can't think of a better definition of magic.

"People are always blaming their circumstances for what they are. I don't believe in circumstances. The people who get on in this world are the people who get up and look for the circumstances they want and if they can't find them, make them."

George Bernard Shaw

Love and
Affection

Love really does make the world go 'round. From teenagers in a lip lock, to old marrieds going bowling on a Friday night, to sisters who talk every day, to the friends who are so close they're really your family, to the kindness of strangers. Love is the best. It's the impetus for the creation of songs, poems, gardens, and more (not to mention babies). It's a reason for long journeys, and it keeps hope alive in the hardest places. The love between two people is a living thing with its own history and hopes, a journey in and of itself. The love in a family nurtures us and keeps us going. The love for humanity inspires generosity, growth, and understanding. And, as they say in all those songs and poems, love never dies. It is a currency that cannot be devalued, a flower that never loses its bloom.

The Love Underneath

Scratch the surface of every good thing in the world, and you'll find love.

Generosity: Love of giving freely

Listening: Love of tuning in

Keeping promises: Love of following through

Understanding: The love underneath it all

Curiosity: Love of knowledge

Justice: Love for fellow human beings

Forgiveness: Love of self

Peace: Love beyond self

Love List

If I'm feeling low, one of the best ways I know to perk up is to make a love list. It's simple, just a list of every single person I love. Then I follow it up with another list, of all the people I know who love me. I can stash it in a pocket to take with me on a tough day, or just keep it in mind as I get on with my life.

Kindred Souls

"Friendship is born at that moment when one person says to another, 'What! You too? I thought I was the only one.'"

C. S. Lewis

Gossiping

I know, I know, your mother was right when she told you not to gossip, but what about a new take on it? Why not get together and have a feel good gossip party, where the "omigosh" is not so much about scandal but about celebration of the great things in your friends' lives.

How to Know if You're Nuts

"The statistics on sanity are that one out of every four Americans is suffering from some form of mental illness. Think of your three best friends. If they're okay, then it's you."

Rita Mae Brown

Spending Time Alone

We all need some time to learn to be alone, whether it feels like it's our own choice or not. There is wonderful possibility in solitude. As Alice Koller said, "Being solitary is being alone well: being alone luxuriously immersed in doings of your own choice, aware of the fullness of your own presence rather than of the absence of others. Because solitude is an achievement."

Other People

Sometimes you'll want to be a loner, and sometimes you'll want to be a joiner: at school, at home, at work, in your neighborhood. You get to decide how to maximize your happiness.

—

Love Is

"Love is the condition
in which the happiness of
another person is essential
to your own."

Robert Heinlein

Comparisons

I've heard people say that you should never compare your-self or your situation to anyone else's. And I do believe that it doesn't do any good to harshly judge your own feelings by comparing your happiness or pain to someone else's. But sometimes it helps to listen to other people's stories, to put your feelings in a broader perspective and to remember that you're not alone, even in your most lonely, desolate moods.

A Complicated Problem

Sometimes we want to keep our problems complicated because we're invested in an image of ourselves in constant struggle with an unbeatable obstacle. Or we're terrified of the solution because it probably requires change on our part, so we convince ourselves it's too complex to solve. Happiness might be closer than you think—try asking for help from someone whose opinion you respect, and really listen to what they say. They might see the bigger picture more clearly, and help you on your way to solving your problem.

Pretending to Be Strangers

Ask your partner to tell you a story from her childhood, or to describe a time in her life that she faced or overcame a fear. Talk like you're just meeting someone—but without any stranger anxiety—a stranger you trust implicitly to share special secrets about your past or the intriguing things about the way you think or relate to the world. Too often we forget to keep "getting to know" our partners because we assume we already know them well enough; it's fun sometimes to start at the beginning.

"Choose thy love. Love thy choice."

German proverb

Off to Bed and Forget the Fight

Maya Angelou's brother gave her a painting with the instruction to hang it so that it was the last thing she and her husband saw before going to bed at night. So if they were in the middle of an argument, they could look at the painting and say, "Oh, stop. Whatever it was, whatever you said, forget it," and go to bed with a twinkle in their eyes.

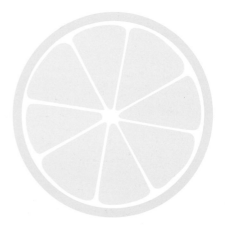

Date Night

Dinner, a movie, pretending you don't have a houseful of kids and their toys for four hours straight. We don't get to do it enough, but I think having a weekly date night with your partner is the one of the best things you can do.

Green and Slimy

"Love is like seaweed;
even if you have pushed it
away, you will not prevent
it from coming back."

Nigerian proverb

Love Letters

Not just for romance, you can write a love letter to almost anyone. Try writing a letter full of love to your favorite aunt, or a writer you admire, or even yourself! You could also send a letter to a perfect stranger who might need some love and support—someone serving in the military, or recovering from a natural disaster, or coping with a loss.

Bonds of Family

How amazing that you belong to a group of people, by blood, by marriage, or by choice. They are your context, your root system, your springboard, and your landing pad. And you are theirs.

Your Kids 2.0

Author, educator, and humorist Sam Levenson said, "The reason grandparents and grandchildren get along so well is that they have a common enemy." It's true, these two are really in cahoots. There's something about grandkids—it's like Your Kids 2.0, and you get another chance to do all the fun stuff and can pretty much opt out of the annoying stuff when you want to.

Aunts, Uncles, and Cousins

I always thought of these as family-lite, in a really good way. Meaning you can let down your guard and be yourself, you can have a ton of fun with them, but because you don't usually live together, you probably don't end up screaming at each other about who used the last squeeze of toothpaste. Maybe they'll let you eat sugar cereal and tell you about the birds and bees, too.

In Memoriam

In a Quaker funeral service, loved ones sit in silence in a circle and speak whenever they feel moved to share thoughts, memories, and inspiration. It is often the greatest comfort when someone has died to remember how they loved and were loved by those around them.

"We cannot do great things
on this earth, only small things
with great love."

Mother Teresa

Passion ignites purpose, and most if not all of the forces for good in this world emanate from love: generosity, understanding, kindness, justice. Most of us are surrounded by more love than we might consciously think about on a day-to-day basis. You're on the receiving end of love that is literally flowing around the globe. Perhaps even better, you're on the giving end of that love, and no matter how much you share, the tank never runs low.

The Only Word We Need

"One word frees us of all
the weight and pain of life:
That word is love."

Sophocles

Love: the most powerful way to join together, to take care of each other, to find courage, to heal wounds, to overcome obstacles, to spread peace, and to find contentment.

Thanksgiving

Every Day

You don't have to wait for the stuffing and cranberry sauce to give heartfelt thanks. You can do it all day, every day. The more the better. There's a ton of medical research to back it up: People who appreciate where their bread is buttered and how sweet the jam on their toast is—well, they're healthier, they live longer, they're usually more successful (although they may not define success as having the most marbles), and for sure other people want to spend more time around them.

Gratitude

Your mother taught you to be polite, to say "Please" and "Thank you," to wait your turn, to share with others. And by now those things are ingrained and you don't even have to think about it to remember to do them. But when's the last time you said "Thank you" out loud for the good things in your life?

Jot It Down

You can be measurably happier if you take the time every night to write down five (or more) things you are thankful for. They can be one word, or longer descriptions, or a combination of both. You have to actually do it—get a little notebook and put it next to the bed and go for it. I know you're tired, but it's worth it. Go get a pen, already!

"There are two ways to live your life.
One is as though nothing is a miracle. The
other is as though everything is a miracle."

Albert Einstein

What to Do with the Overflow

What a wonderful feeling when your cup runneth over. For whatever reason, the bounty is beyond your expectation. You've got a ton of leftovers from Thanksgiving dinner, your cousin is cleaning out her closet that's full of designer clothes, or you got an unexpected year-end bonus at work. My first impulse is to save some for a rainy day, which is all to the good, but not at the expense of using it well or passing some on.

Use It Up

What's the point in hoarding (especially where leftovers are concerned)? Throw a big party to share your excess, and bask in glory of it all.

Give It Away

If it makes you feel good to have a little extra, imagine those feelings radiating out into the world when you pass it on.

All Used Up

"I want to be thoroughly used up when I die,
for the harder I work, the more I live.
I rejoice in life for its own sake. Life is
no 'brief candle' to me. It is a sort of
splendid torch which I have got hold of
for the moment, and I want to make it
burn as brightly as possible before
handing it on to future generations."

George Bernard Shaw

Out on a Limb

Here's to all the people in the world whose passion and persistence take them to the edge of something new. And here's to finding the courage to jump. And here's to flying for the first time.

Ambition Versus Passion

Ambition is the desire to be successful. Passion is intense interest or enthusiasm. My ambition can take me far—it can motivate me to make it to the top. But the end result may feel pretty empty when I get there, because the goal was seeing myself as a success, and once I've done that, what's left? Passion, on the other hand, is ready to explore infinite possibilities. It may or may not lead me to someone else's definition of success, but following my passion elicits a sense of fulfillment that can never grow dull.

"Things that were
hard to bear are sweet
to remember."

Seneca

Pace Yourself

Why is it that we rush through the good stuff (hugs, walking the dog, home-cooked meals) and linger over the not so good (reading bad news in the paper, procrastinating about getting the car fixed)? Time to reset the internal speedometer.

The Family You Choose

I don't know what I'd do without my friends, old and new. If your family is perfectly normal and never forces you to pretend you don't know them in a restaurant, I envy you. Don't get me wrong, I wouldn't trade my band of crazies for anything in the world, but sometimes I need some time off. That's why I've got my chosen family—the godparents, aunties, and best friends who might as well be blood relations—to step in and save the day. They do, and for that I will always be grateful.

Winning Big

Balance is the key to good health and a good life. We do best when we're able to weigh doing what we love against doing what's good for us, and we've hit the jackpot when we can do things as often as possible that are rewarding in the moment as well as later on.

Permission to Enjoy What You've Got

No matter what you don't have, or what you think you need, never forget what you've already got and what a source of joy it can be to reinvest yourself in discovering and enjoying what's all around you all the time. Grant yourself permission to notice your own happiness

To Our Readers

Conari Press, an imprint of Red Wheel/Weiser, publishes books on topics ranging from spirituality, personal growth, and relationships to women's issues, parenting, and social issues. Our mission is to publish quality books that will make a difference in people's lives—how we feel about ourselves and how we relate to one another. We value integrity, compassion, and receptivity, both in the books we publish and in the way we do business.

Our readers are our most important resource, and we value your input, suggestions, and ideas about what you would like to see published. Please feel free to contact us, to request our latest book catalog, or to be added to our mailing list.

Conari Press

An imprint of Red Wheel/Weiser, LLC

500 Third Street, Suite 230

San Francisco, CA 94107

www.redwheelweiser.com